Stencil It!

D0731068

Camden House

Kids' Projects by Sandra Buckingham

Canadian Cataloguing in Publication Data

Buckingham, Sandra, 1944-
   Stencil it! : kids' projects

ISBN 0-921820-75-5 (lib. bdg.)
ISBN 0-921820-73-9 (pbk.)

1. Stencil work - Juvenile literature.   I. Title.

NK8654.B8 1993   j745.7'3   C93-094509-3

Published by Camden House Publishing
(a division of Telemedia Communications Inc.)

Camden House Publishing
7 Queen Victoria Road
Camden East, Ontario K0K 1J0

Camden House Publishing
Box 766
Buffalo, New York 14240-0766

Trade distribution by
Firefly Books
250 Sparks Avenue
Willowdale, Ontario
Canada M2H 2S4

Box 1325
Ellicott Station
Buffalo, New York 14205

Design by
Linda J. Menyes

Photography by
Ernie Sparks

Demonstration by
Allison Good

Filmwork by
Hadwen Graphics Limited
Ottawa, Ontario

Printed and bound in Canada by
D.W. Friesen & Sons
Altona, Manitoba

page 56 top: Lascaux (Dordogne) Cheval LS 16, Jean Vertut/Yvonne Vertut, Issy les Moulineaux, France
   page 56 bottom: Lascaux (Dordogne) LS cerf LS 13, Jean Vertut/Yvonne Vertut, Issy les Moulineaux, France
   page 46 top: MATISSE, Henri. *Destiny*, plate XVI from *Jazz* by Henri Matisse. Paris, E. Tériade, 1947. Pochoir, printed in colour, double sheet 16⁵/₈'' x 25⁵/₈''. The Museum of Modern Art, New York. The Louis E. Stern Collection
   page 46 bottom: MATISSE, Henri. *The Codomas*, plate XI from *Jazz* by Henri Matisse. Paris, E. Tériade, 1947. Pochoir, printed in colour, double sheet 16⁵/₈'' x 25⁵/₈''. The Museum of Modern Art, New York. The Louis E. Stern Collection

To my mother,
Bernice Patricia Birnie,
and to my nana,
Annie Matilda Smith

Contents

Getting Started

"Me??? Paint a T-shirt? You're kidding! . . . I can't even draw."

Sound familiar? Well, if you think that you're not great at art and are convinced that you can't draw to save your life, stencilling may be just the skill you need. And if you *can* draw—if you live, think and breathe art—then you'll find stencilling is a wonderful addition to your painting techniques.

Painting? Wait a minute. How can you "paint" a stencil? Doesn't the paint run under the edge of the stencil and make a sticky mess?

Well, yes, it can. If your brush is dripping with paint and you paint the way you normally would, it will make an incredible mess. But when you stencil, you use a dry brush and so little paint that there's none left over to run under the stencil.

So, What's a Stencil?

Each of the cutouts in this photograph is actually a stencil. A stencil is nothing more than a piece of paper or plastic or metal or, depending on where you live, a sealskin or a banana leaf with a design cut out of it. The design can be any shape you choose—a snail or a star or a snapping turtle. If you lay the stencil against a wall or on a T-shirt or a piece of paper and paint over it, you can create your own work of art.

We're going to use stencils to paint all sorts of neat images on everything from birthday cards to baseball caps to bedroom walls. You don't have to be "good at art," because you can copy the patterns in this book to make your own stencils. You'll be amazed at how wonderful your work looks, even if you haven't managed to cut the stencil perfectly.

Much of what you will need you can probably find around the house.

Stencil Material: Freezer paper, overhead-projector film, an old vinyl tablecloth or even thin cardboard (a used file folder) can each be used as stencil material. The material should be flat and easy to cut, and it shouldn't let paint through. Freezer paper is probably the least expensive and the easiest material to work with, and it's what we use throughout this book. It is a brown or white paper coated on one side with a thin film of plastic. You can buy it by the roll at your super-market. If the plastic side is not on the outside of the roll, reroll it so that it is. It is much easier to use that way.

Paint: You can use almost any-thing that isn't too watery—acrylic paint (tubes or jars), fabric paint (great for paper too) or latex house paint. Poster and disk paints work, but they sometimes make the stencils curl.

Paint Applicators: Stencil brushes, which are short and stubby with a full head of bristles, foam rollers, sponges and toothbrushes (for spattering).

Spray Adhesive: Spraying low-tack glue on the back of a stencil makes stencilling easier. It keeps the stencil in place and the wiggly parts from flopping around. The new glue sticks for making Post-it Notes also work.

Miscellaneous: Small scissors or an X-acto knife; cardboard; a perma-nent felt-tipped pen or a pencil; a plastic ice-cream lid or a styrofoam tray; a rag or some paper towels.

Although today's spray glues should be environmentally safe, they still contain chemicals that are dangerous if inhaled, so spray your stencils outdoors. A light spray on the back of each stencil is all you will need. One spray should last as long as the stencil. Let the glue dry before using.

Spray over sheets of newspaper so that nothing else will get glue on it. If you spray something you didn't mean to, ask an adult to wipe the surface with a rag and a touch of paint thinner.

Finally, remember to check the direction of spray before pressing the button—you don't want to spray yourself in the face. Adults should always do the spraying for young children.

An X-acto knife cannot cut sten-cils if the blade is dull, so be sure you have fresh blades on hand. These blades are razor-sharp, however, and must be handled with extreme care. Always keep them capped and stored in a safe place. Small children should *never* use X-acto knives.

Protect the surface of your worktable when you are using an X-acto knife by working over a cutting board or a sheet of firm cardboard.

Since all the paints used in this book are water-based, you won't need anything more than soap and water for cleaning up.

How to Make a Stencil

The really great part about stencilling is that you don't have to be able to draw. If you see a design you like —on fabric, in a magazine or on a poster—trace an outline of it on a piece of paper. That outline becomes your pattern. To make the pattern bigger (or smaller) than it was originally, use the enlarger/reducer option on a photocopier.

If you can't get to a photocopier, there is another way to increase the size of a pattern. Draw a grid of horizontal and vertical lines over the pattern. On a second piece of paper, draw a bigger grid. Then, square by square, copy the pattern onto the larger grid.

If you're stuck for a design to start with, photocopy or trace the birds below to use as your pattern.

Cutting With Scissors

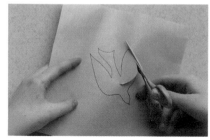

Cut out a square of freezer paper slightly bigger than your design. With the pattern centred underneath, hold it up to the window. Trace an outline of the pattern onto the freezer paper with a permanent felt-tipped pen. To start cutting, poke a tiny hole inside the pattern with your scissors. Then cut out the shape.

Cutting With an X-acto Knife

1 Lightly spray the back of the pattern with glue. Press the sticky side of the pattern onto the shiny side of a piece of freezer paper.

2 Hold the X-acto knife firmly, and press the tip along the outline of the pattern, cutting through both the pattern and the freezer paper.

3 When you have finished, cover the blade of your knife and put it safely away. Carefully peel the pattern off the freezer paper.

1 Place the stencil right side down (for freezer paper, this is the shiny side) on newspaper. Apply a tiny bit of spray glue to the back of the stencil.

2 Put the stencil shiny side up on a piece of paper or a greeting card. Smooth it down so that it is lying flat on the paper.

Put some paint in one corner of an ice-cream lid or a styrofoam tray. Next to it, put a small piece of moist sponge for dampening your brush when it gets too dry. Dab a tiny amount of paint on the end of a dry stencil brush. Work the paint in evenly by rubbing the brush in circles on the tray. Wipe the brush on a dry rag to get rid of any extra paint. Your brush should feel almost dry.

1 After working the paint into the bristles, hold the brush straight up and down. Paint the stencil by rubbing the bristles around in circles.

2 You can also apply paint by dabbing the brush straight up and down, or "stippling." Wrap the bristles with masking tape to keep them firm.

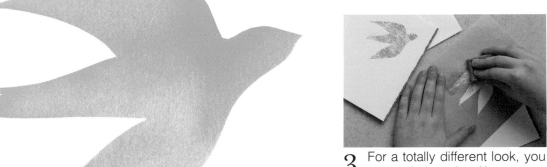

3 For a totally different look, you can apply the paint with a sponge or a foam dabber. (Remember: Don't use too much paint.)

Greeting Cards

Mass Production

Framed!

Whose cards stay displayed on the refrigerator door forever? Yours, of course, when you give cards you make yourself. Start with blank cards cut and folded from sheet paper—be sure the cards will fit into the envelopes you're using. If you're making invitations for a huge birthday party or cards for your family's Christmas list, you will need a simple card holder with a hinged stencil to make mass production faster and easier.

By recycling paper from shopping bags and lunch bags, you can also create wrapping paper for all your gifts. I use rollers and vivid latex paint to make beautiful gift wrap. Just stick the stencil down, paint, sponge or spatter it, lift it up, move it over, stick it down, and keep on going. Don't waste time lining up the patterns. Scatter the prints randomly.

1 Glue narrow strips of thin cardboard at right angles along two sides of a larger piece of cardboard. Push a card into the corner.

2 Spray a little glue onto the back of the stencil. Place the stencil on the card. Tape the stencil to the guide so that it is hinged on one side.

3 Paint the card. Lift the stencil, and take out the printed card. Push a new card into the corner, lower the stencil, and paint. Repeat.

Creating a frame for your print will give your card a special look. First, stencil your designs onto small pieces of paper. Then mount them on slightly larger pieces of coloured paper. Once you've put those pieces together, you can glue the whole thing to the front of a blank card.

For a straight edge on the background paper, tear the paper along the edge of a ruler. For a completely clean edge, use scissors. For an uneven edge, tear it by hand.

1 You can mix and match various paper types and shapes. Place torn paper on torn paper, and position your stencil at different angles.

2 Add a number of borders to your prints by mounting them on layers of cut paper. Again, try placing the layers at different angles.

The fastest way to transform a roll of kraft paper into enough Christmas wrapping for the entire family is to use foam rollers. Don't use nap rollers, because they hold too much paint. The secret of stencilling with foam rollers is to use very little paint and to get that small bit of paint spread evenly on the roller. With roller stencilling, you can use latex house paint, so it's very inexpensive. Your family probably has cans of leftover paint sitting in the basement.

3 Before painting the stencil, work the roller over a folded rag, a stack of scrap paper or paper towels to remove the excess paint.

When your print looks like this, it means the paint on the roller is uneven. To avoid this, work the paint out on your tray or paper towels.

1 Put a few spoonfuls of paint at one end of a styrofoam tray. Using a Popsicle stick, spread this puddle into a thin layer over the tray.

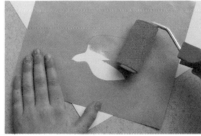

4 Smooth the stencil onto your practice paper. Move the roller over it a few times—lightly at first, in case there is still too much paint on it.

If your print looks like this—all wobbly and blurry at the edges—then your roller or brush either has too much paint or is too wet. Work as much paint as you can onto rags or paper towels before making another print. Wipe off the back of the stencil too, because some of the paint will have seeped under it.

Important: If you wet the roller or brush too much, paint will run under your stencil. Instead, when your roller or brush gets too dry to make a good print, dampen it by wiping it on a moist sponge. If you want to change colours, you need a fresh, dry brush or roller for each new colour.

2 Pull the roller through this layer. Work the roller back and forth on a piece of freezer paper until the paint is evenly spread on the roller.

5 Lift a corner of the stencil to see whether the paint on the print is dark enough. If it isn't, roll it once more, pressing a little harder.

Beyond Silhouettes

Looking for something a little more thrilling than a plain silhouette? Nothing could be easier. You can add excitement with colour, shadows and pattern. Let's start with something that grows and dies every year, comes in a thousand different shapes and can't help changing colours. There are hundreds of them every fall in your backyard or on the playground. Leaves make great stencils, because you can trace or photocopy them from nature—you don't have to "think of something to draw." The shapes are easy to cut out with scissors or an X-acto knife, and they look terrific when printed. The small indentations and sharp points show up perfectly. Whether you're printing the lobes of a leaf or the fangs of a werewolf, there's nothing like a stencil for making all those little points look crisp.

Colour and Shadow

Spatter Painting

Stencils With Bridges

Brighten up a silhouette by using two or more colours and blending or spattering them. Or use transparent paint so that the shadows of overlapping silhouettes show through. You need a separate brush for each colour—rinsing a brush between applications leaves it too wet. Using the same stencil for different colours may produce muddy results, so keep more stencils on hand for colour changes. To make extras, stack several layers of freezer paper (a little spray glue on the underside of each piece will prevent slipping) and cut through all the layers at the same time.

Use a stencil to paint a leaf. Before lifting the stencil, dip a toothbrush into a different colour of paint, hold the brush over the stencil, and drag a Popsicle stick over the bristles. Pull the stick toward you so that the paint spatters on the paper, not on you.

You can add detail to a very basic leaf shape by leaving "bridges," or "ties," in the stencil that correspond with the pattern of veins in real leaves. This kind of complicated stencil is much easier to cut out with an X-acto knife than with scissors.

Stationery

This stationery set was made from plain brown recycled paper. It has been decorated with a simple leaf stencil, painted over and over in a random pattern. The transparent fabric paint used here lets overlapping shapes show through, as though sunlight were shining through the leaves. Fabric paint works well on paper—it goes on more smoothly than acrylic paint. A light coat of acrylic varnish will protect much-handled paper objects. Let the paint dry several days before varnishing.

1 In addition to bridges, there is another way to create patterns within a silhouette. First, stencil the shape with a solid colour—we're using black on these turtles. Leave the stencil in place.

2 To keep the turtle's feet, head and tail solid black, cover them with either Post-it Notes or little squares of spray-glued paper.

3 Now, take a stencil with polka dots, zigzags or random shapes and stick it down on top of the turtle pattern. Paint this stencil with a bright colour. If it is too transparent to show up over black, then use a lighter colour for the turtle silhouette.

1 Sometimes, you may want the stripes or diamonds to follow the shape of the animal. Here's one way to do it. Stencil the basic shape first.

2 The second stencil has some hinged cutouts, or flaps. Carefully line up the snake's head and tail with these cutouts.

3 Press the flaps down so that the head and the tip of the tail are covered. Apply the second colour through the stripe-and-eye stencil.

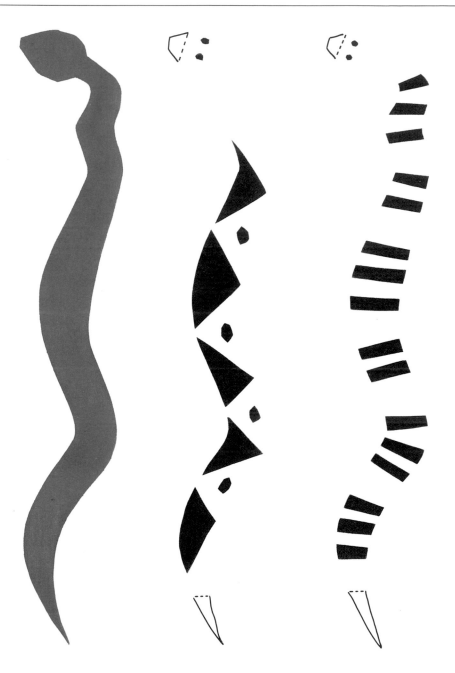

Colour and More Colour

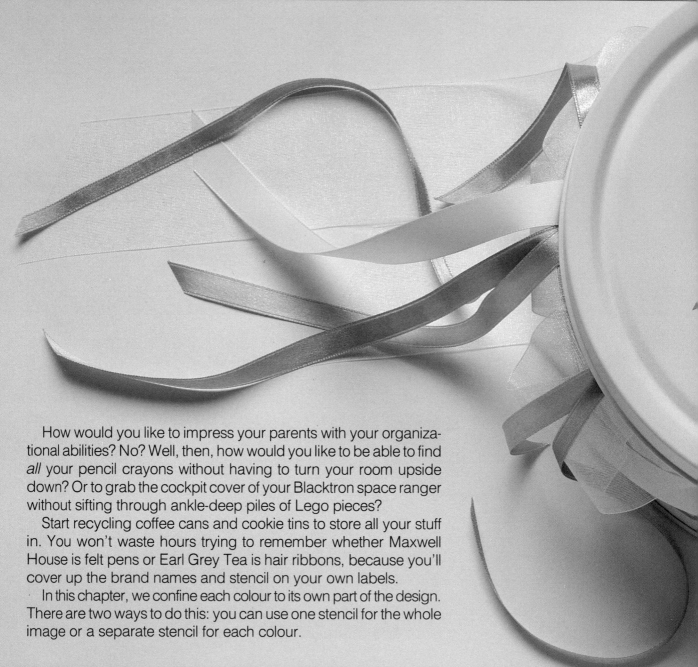

How would you like to impress your parents with your organizational abilities? No? Well, then, how would you like to be able to find *all* your pencil crayons without having to turn your room upside down? Or to grab the cockpit cover of your Blacktron space ranger without sifting through ankle-deep piles of Lego pieces?

Start recycling coffee cans and cookie tins to store all your stuff in. You won't waste hours trying to remember whether Maxwell House is felt pens or Earl Grey Tea is hair ribbons, because you'll cover up the brand names and stencil on your own labels.

In this chapter, we confine each colour to its own part of the design. There are two ways to do this: you can use one stencil for the whole image or a separate stencil for each colour.

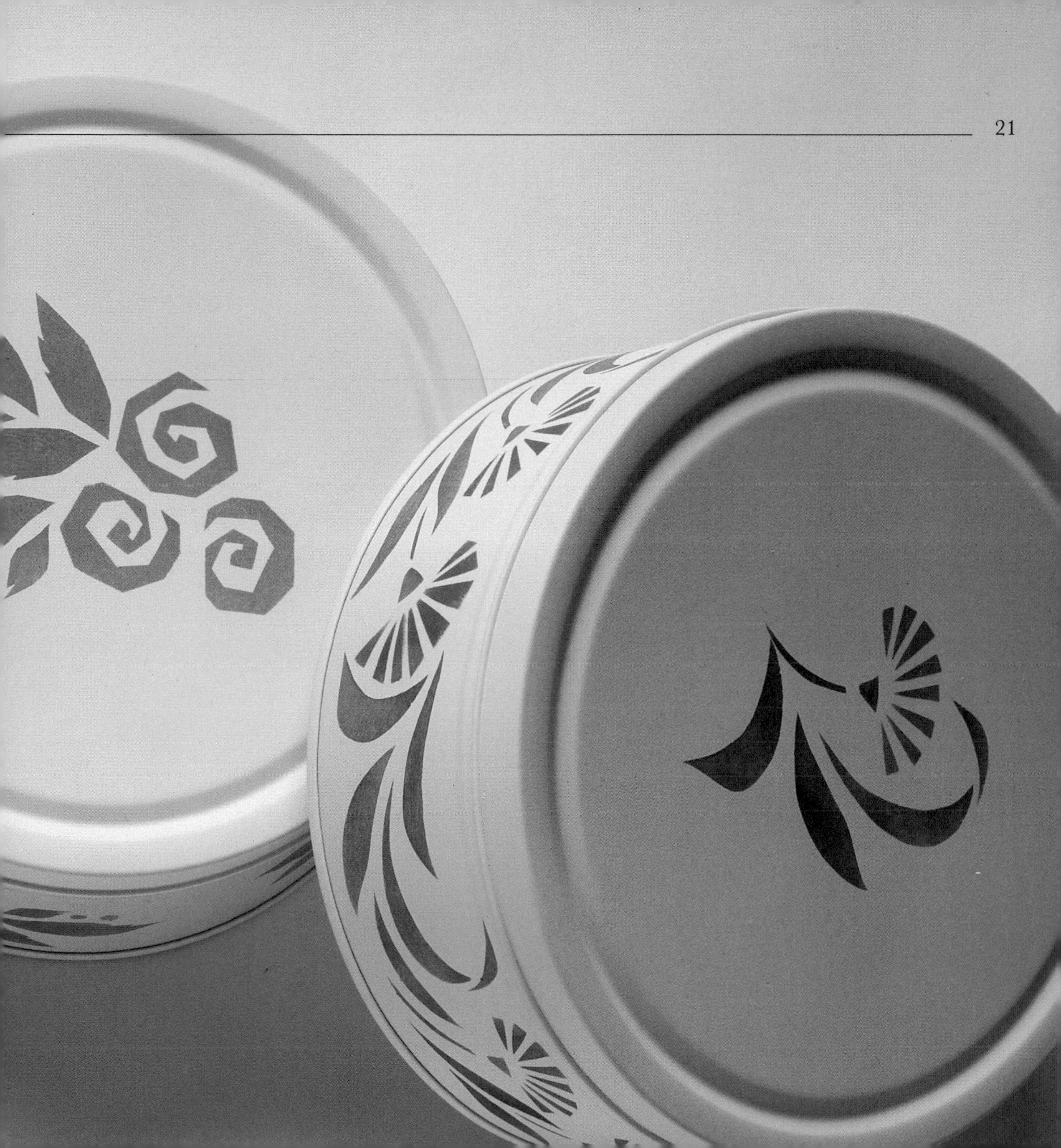

1 With the first method, the whole design appears on one stencil. Paint the leaves green. Some of the green may blur over onto the flower.

2 Without moving the stencil, use a fresh brush to paint the flower pink. Again, some of the paint will smudge over onto the leaves.

3 Lift the stencil carefully. You can now see how the green colour blends into the pink colour where the leaf meets the flower.

1 In this exercise, we are using two stencils—a separate stencil for each colour. Position the leaf stencil, and paint it green.

2 Line up the flaps on either side of the flower with the painted leaf tips. Press the stencil in place. Paint the flower.

3 In this print, there is no overlapping of colours. Both the flower and the leaf colours are confined to their own areas.

1 Go outside, and put the tin on newspaper. Cover it evenly with acrylic spray paint (nonglossy). Follow the instructions on the spray can.

2 Trim the stencil to fit, wrap it around the tin, and press it in place. Protect the bottom edge of the tin with a strip of masking tape.

3 Stencil the flowers with acrylic paint. Remember to use very little paint. If you want the flower to look darker, add a second coat.

Material World

Have you ever painted a T-shirt that didn't turn out at all the way you had imagined? You're never going to wear it, and you're not going to try again, because you wasted 10 dollars on the first shirt and maybe a second one won't turn out any better . . . .

Well, here's an idea with no risk! Stencil your designs onto small squares of cotton cloth, then sew the patches onto shirts, hats or pockets. They can be like labels on a shirt or badges on a sleeve. Scatter more than one over the front of a sweat shirt. You can either hem them neatly or fray the edges.

Because you know ahead of time exactly what the design will look like, stencilling gives you a built-in safety margin. And if something does go wrong, all you're wasting is a small piece of cloth.

You can use fabric paint, acrylic paint or latex paint to stencil cloth. There are many different brands, so start with whatever is handy, then try others to see what works best. Fabric paints dry soft and don't stiffen the cloth. To make fabric paint laundry-proof, follow the directions on the paint label. The label may also have washing instructions. Acrylic and latex paints can make the fabric feel a little stiff, but when they have dried for about a week, they should be permanent.

Always test your paints on pieces of scrap fabric first to make sure they are washable.

Before you start any project, wash, dry and iron your fabric.

1 To create a work surface that doesn't slip, cut a piece of cardboard from a cereal box, and spray one side very lightly with glue.

2 Smooth the cloth patch onto the sticky side of the cardboard. Lightly spray glue on the back of the stencil, then place it over the patch.

3 You can apply the paint with a brush, a sponge or a roller. A brush gives the sharpest print. Use it with a circular scrubbing motion.

4 To add dazzle to your project, leave the stencil in place, and using a small, flat brush, carefully apply some sparkle paint.

5 You can add bumpy eyes, dots or other details with dimensional paint by simply squeezing out dabs through the applicator tip.

1 If you use fabric paint, follow the directions on the container. You may have to press the back of the fabric with a hot iron to make the paint permanent.

2 To finish your patch, either fold a little hem along each edge of the square and press it under or pull out the threads along all four edges to create a fringe.

3 Pin, baste and machine-stitch the patch in place. Use a zigzag stitch along frayed edges so that they won't keep fraying. You can also use fusible webbing to iron on the patch.

How do you stencil an even row of spiders along a bandanna? On paper, draw a line for the hemmed edge. Trace two identical spiders along the line. Using this as a pattern, cut a stencil of the spiders. Cut notches at both ends of the line. The notches and one of the spiders are used to line up the stencil for each repeat print. Paint the other spider.

1 Place the bandanna on a spray-glued piece of cardboard. Line up the notches on the stencil with the hem of the bandanna.

2 When you have lined up the stencil, paint the right-hand spider, being careful not to get paint on the left-hand spider.

3 Lift the stencil off the bandanna. Move it over so that the spider you have just painted lines up with the left-hand spider on the stencil.

4 With the notches on the hem and the painted spider peeking through the left-hand cutout, paint the spider stencil on the right again.

5 Complete the bandanna. Near the end of the row, you may have to change the spacing so that you won't finish with a partial spider.

The easiest way to make an all-over design is simply to paint a stencil in random positions. There may be times, though, when you would like to repeat a print with even spacing. Here's how to make a scarf with a regular grid of dragonflies.

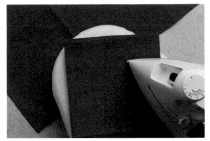

1 Fold the scarf until it is a rectangle that is big enough to contain the shape of the dragonfly. Press the creases with an iron.

2 The creases divide the scarf into even rectangles. Make lines or notches (or both) on the stencil to show where the fabric creases line up.

3 It's often hard to make paint show up on dark fabric. One way is to stencil each motif in white first. Then stencil the final colour on top.

4 Stencil the second dragonfly motif over the corners of the rectangles. Again, use lines or notches to match the creases in the scarf.

Wearable Art

With a bit of paint and a little imagination, you can take something really ordinary—a used denim jacket, a plain T-shirt or even cotton socks—and turn it into something cool. Wearable art lets you make your own statement. It also guarantees that what you're wearing is a ''designer original.''

There are two problems in stencilling what you wear. One is keeping the fabric from stretching. That can be solved by smoothing the fabric onto a spray-glued surface or ironing it onto the shiny side of a piece of freezer paper. The other is getting your object flat and smooth. The answer here is to stuff, stretch and otherwise mess around with the item until a part of it is flat enough to stick a stencil to and firm enough to work on with your brush.

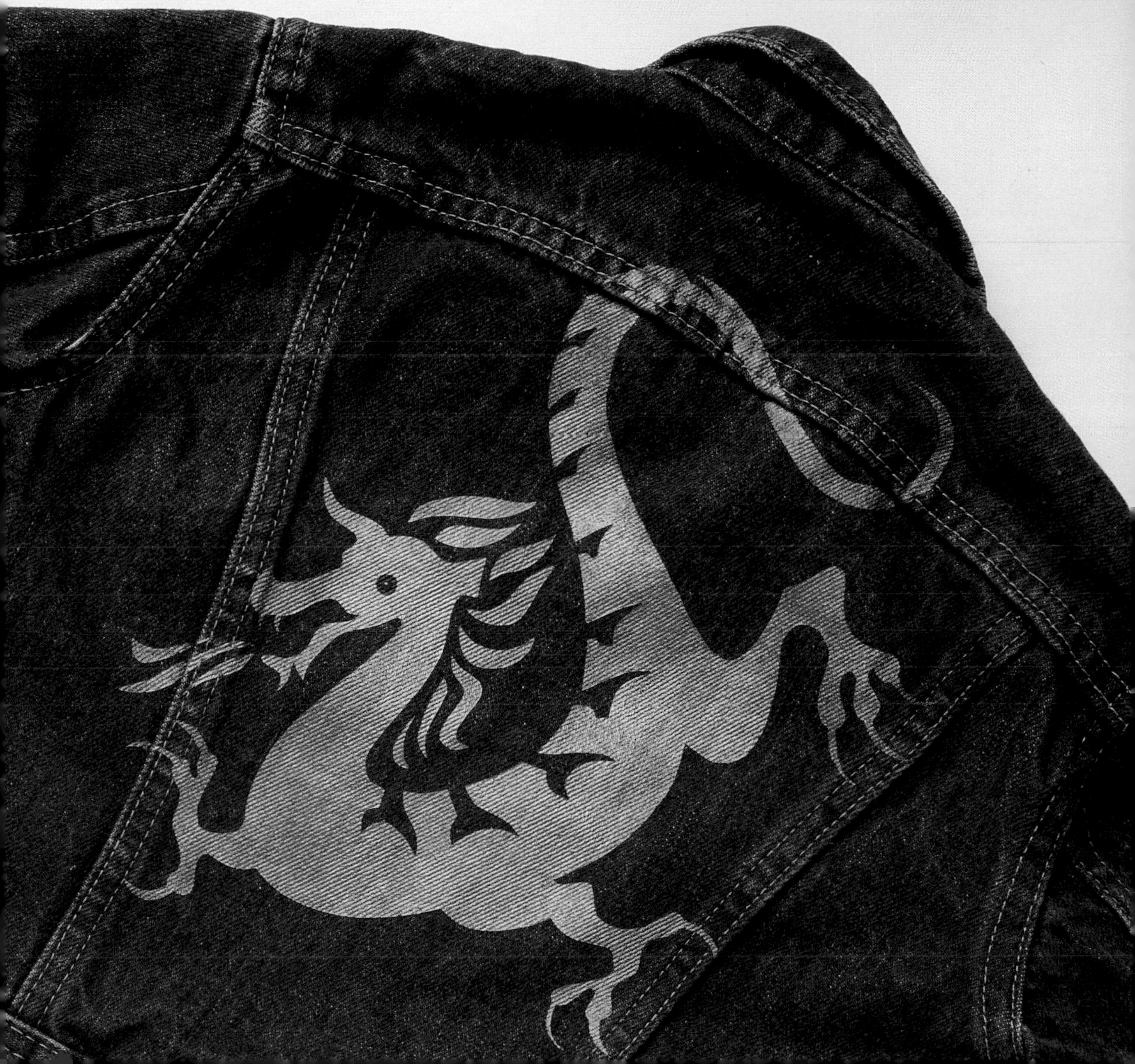

A piece of spray-glued cardboard slipped inside a T-shirt anchors the fabric; so does freezer paper ironed shiny side up to the inside of the shirt.

To make a stiffener that fits, trace one of the socks onto a piece of cardboard. The cardboard will stretch the sock and keep it flat.

Stencilling a big design onto something such as a jacket, which has lumps and bumps and won't lie completely flat, can be a little tricky. Here, we piled a stack of books under the back of the jacket so that the shoulders, arms and collar could fall free, letting the back lie flat. Enlarge the dragon to fit your own jacket, then cut the stencil, and spray it with glue. (If you don't have spray glue, position the stencil with the shiny side down and iron it onto the fabric.) Apply metallic paint sparingly, adding extra coats if necessary. This is a wobbly stencil, so work slowly. Add a dab of dimensional paint for the eye.

To stencil a T-shirt pocket, slip a piece of spray-glued cardboard inside the pocket. The material will stick to it, rather than slide around.

Any round, firm object—a bowl, for instance—can be placed inside a baseball cap to provide a hard surface for stencilling.

Find a clean block of wood that you can slip into a knapsack pocket before you stencil it. It will provide a flat, hard work surface.

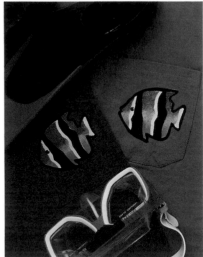

T-shirt fabric is so stretchy, it's almost impossible to stencil without sticking it to something. You can smooth the fabric over spray-glued cardboard or iron it to the shiny side of freezer paper. Stencil the goldfish with gold paint. Then, without removing the stencil, brush on some sparkle paint with a small, flat paintbrush. You'll need three stencils to complete the tropical fish shown below.

You can either trace the lip patterns shown here or ask your mother, if she wears lipstick, to press her lips against a piece of paper, and use those lips as a pattern instead.

A sticky stencil and some masking tape help keep the stencil fixed to an odd-shaped object. Trim the margins of the stencil to make it as small as possible. Remember: Small designs are easier to stencil onto very curved things, such as baseball caps.

Letter Perfect

The school project is due in two weeks, and you get extra marks for an original cover. What about the lettering? When I was in school, there was only one way to do titles: You used a cardboard alphabet stencil to outline the words with a pen, letter by letter.

The packing-crate style of alphabet stencils is a product of what I call ''the donut rule''—as in, you can't stencil a donut. Try it, and see what happens. Right! The middle falls out. The solution is to break up the donut part of letters. You can fill in a B, put a lightning bolt through an O, chop off part of a Q and divide an R into stripes. Or you can do what we do here, and stencil the background behind the letters. This gets rid of the problem, because you stencil the donut holes instead of the donut itself.

1 Draw thick letters with a fat magic marker, using graph paper to help you keep the tops and bottoms of the letters straight.

2 With a pencil, shade in the "negative" areas around the type. By "negative," we mean the area that surrounds the letters.

3 Spray glue lightly onto the back of the graph paper. Then stick the graph paper onto the shiny side of a piece of freezer paper.

4 Carefully cut out all the shaded areas. The P and the O don't fall apart, because we cut out the centre, not the letters themselves.

5 When you peel away the graph paper, you see the freezer paper in the shape of letters and the cutouts in the shape of the background.

Everyone will know it's your book if the first page has your personal bookplate on it, stencilled, of course. Design your own label, using your initials, your name or even a special symbol. Experiment with colours and shading. Before you apply the stencil, you can paint the rectangle that goes under it with a lighter colour or with a mixture of colours.

WARP

SPEED

INTO

OUTER

SPACE

Limited Editions

Matisse did it. Picasso did it. Inuit in Canada's Far North do it. And so can you.

Do what?

Make your own art prints—using stencils! The process is easy, it's inexpensive, and the results are superb. However, you may have to adapt your style. For example, shapes must be precise; they can't "melt" into one another. But as long as you stick to bold, simple designs (and avoid donut shapes), stencil printing will give you results as good as or even better than any other process.

Why? Because the colouring of each stencil cutout is done by hand. The paint can be rubbed, brushed, dabbed, spattered or shaded, creating a varied texture that makes each print an original.

Kate Langdale

1/10

S. Buckingham

1/5

Stencil printing became popular in France at the end of the 1800s, when it was used as a way of copying book illustrations. By the early 1900s, many modern artists in Paris were creating their own stencil works. The most famous of these was Henri Matisse, whose publisher decided that only this kind of printing could capture the bold colours of the artist's cutout artwork in his book *Jazz*. Two famous works from this book appear on this page, and you can use them for inspiration in your own stencilling career.

By the 1930s, more technical methods were being used, and stencil craftspeople had mostly disappeared. There was an interesting exception in Canada's Far North, however. In the 1950s, a young Canadian artist named James Houston watched Inuit women on Baffin Island decorate garments with shapes cut from sealskin. The leftover pieces, with their cutouts, reminded him of stencils, so he experimented with this method when he taught printmaking techniques to Inuit artists.

Lining It Up

1 Draw a pattern. Sketch in the colours. Draw a triangle in each corner of the page. These are for registering, or lining up, each stencil.

4 Cut out each #1 piece. When the #1 sections have been cut out, tape the pattern pieces back in place. Label this stencil #1.

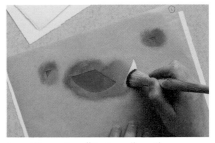

7 Place the #1 stencil on the paper that will hold your final print, and paint the first colour and the registration triangles.

2 You need one stencil for each colour, unless there is a gap between colours. Number each section to show which stencil it is on.

5 Carefully peel off the paper pattern, and stick it onto a second piece of freezer paper. Label this piece stencil #2.

8 You now have four points that will allow you to position the other stencils in the right spot. Line up the #2 stencil with the triangles.

3 Spray glue onto the back of the pattern, and stick it onto a piece of freezer paper. Carefully cut out and remove the registration triangles.

6 Cut out the triangles and the #2 pieces. Tape them back in place before you peel off the pattern. Repeat procedure for each stencil.

9 Work through each different stencil, lining them up as you go, until you have filled in all the colours of your original design.

Sometimes, the scraps of paper that are left over after you cut out a stencil look too good to discard. So instead of throwing them out, recycle them for a brand-new project. Spray glue onto the back of the scraps, and use them like stickers. Put them onto paper or fabric, and run a roller over them. Peel off the stickers, and you have a perfect image on a painted background. Try roller painting over stickers and stencils together to create abstract paintings.

1 Stick the cutout dragon onto a piece of paper. Spatter the page with dots of gold paint, then roll on an uneven coat of red paint.

2 When you peel off the dragon cutout, you will see an animated creature dancing through fiery lava and molten globs of gold.

For special effects with a paint roller, it's hard to beat torn paper. Tear some freezer paper into long, uneven strips, spray them with glue, and stick them onto your work-of-art-to-be. Roll some colour over the spaces between the strips. Lift the strips, move them, and repeat. Stencil some leaves before and after you do this. Veins of colour will pass under and over the leaves.

Another trick is to trim the edge of the stencil fairly close to the leaf cutout. Roll paint over the cutout and over the edge of the stencil, producing a painted frame or halo around the leaf. Create a more interesting halo shape by tearing the edges of the stencil. Make repeat overlapping prints to build up an abstract design.

Paint right to the edge of the paper so that some of the stencils continue over the edge. If you prefer a neat, blank margin, just cut a big rectangle out of freezer paper, and stick it, centred, onto your paper before you start. Leave it there until you're finished, then peel it off.

By playing around with colour, painting techniques and the way you combine shapes, you can create a fantastic-looking T-shirt—a kind of movable work of art. Try rolling and spattering paint. Use a blend of colours instead of just one. Overlap your shapes so that they seem to move, and use a big square stencil on your T-shirt to keep your masterpiece within a neat window.

1 Cut out squiggly shapes, spray them with glue, and stick them onto the T-shirt. Roll over these "stickers" with unevenly mixed paint.

2 Peel off the stickers, leaving the window, and with a toothbrush dipped in acrylic paint, make random spatters across the square area.

3 Using a brush and black acrylic paint, stencil stick people across the shirt, letting the figures overlap and leap out beyond the window.

A Place of One's Own

No one understood why my 4-year-old nephew hated the wallpaper in his room. Everyone else loved it. With its old-fashioned trains and steam engines, it looked like a magazine-perfect boy's room.

What Kirk really wanted was bunny rabbits. His mom explained to him that he would soon outgrow them and that he would get used to the trains. But for as long as they lived in that house, my nephew avoided his room, and he never went to bed without a fight.

"That wallpaper terrified me," he remembered years later. "In the dark, with a shaft of moonlight shining through the window, each locomotive looked like a snarling wolf leaping out of the wall. But I was too embarrassed to tell anyone." Then, as he headed off to campus, he added with a grin: "And I still like bunny rabbits."

Most of us long for a place to call our own, a place where we can get away from the rest of the world for a while. But unless you can choose what goes in it and how it looks, that place is not truly yours. With simple stencils and a little paint, it's easy to create your own space. It doesn't even have to be a whole room—it could be a corner or a little alcove under the stairs. You can even decorate the inside of your closet.

We've transformed this bedroom wall into a romantic retreat—perfect for reading or daydreaming on a rainy afternoon.

1 For this project, you'll need to wear rubber gloves. Pour some paint into a tray, dip a rag into the paint, and rub it onto a white wall in a circular motion. The colour should be uneven, like a cloudy night sky.

2 Cut star stencils from a simple pattern, and with the shiniest gold paint you can find, scatter different-sized stars over your sky.

Inspiration

What do you do when you can't think of anything to draw or paint? Just look around you for inspiration—there are hundreds of things in your everyday life to use as subjects. You can paint something the way it really looks, the way you feel it looks or the way it makes you feel. Look at shadows changing shape as they move over smooth and uneven ground, at leaves fluttering in the wind and falling, at sunlight shining through the petals of a flower. Look at birds and insects, at their colours and patterns. Inspiration comes simply from observing what is around you or within you. Ancient humans, too, looked around themselves and within themselves. They even explored their dreams. What they recorded in colours of the earth was sometimes realistic, sometimes primitive, often mystical.

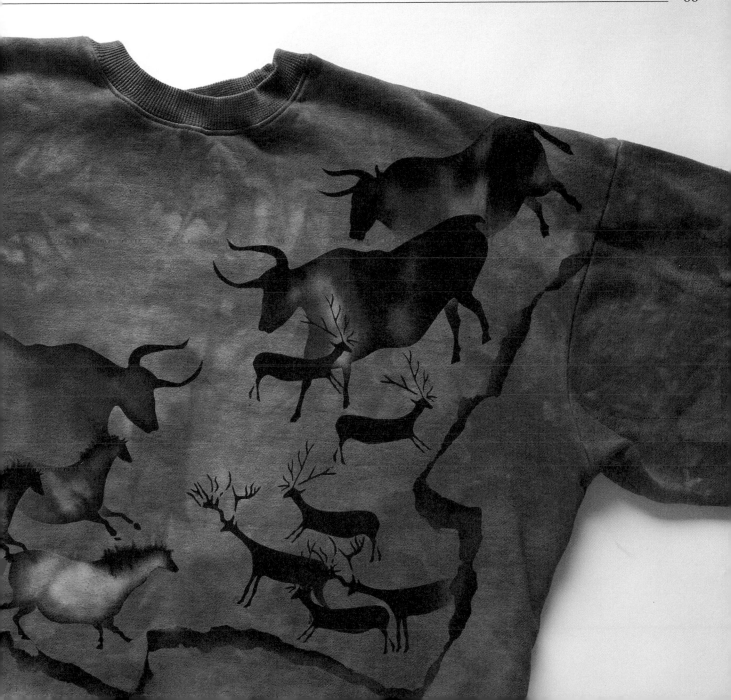

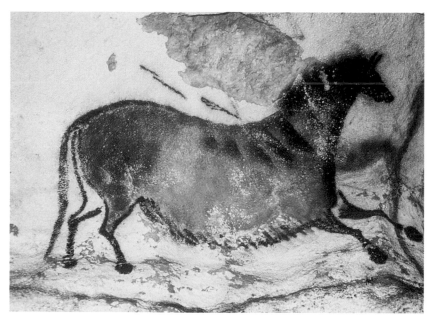

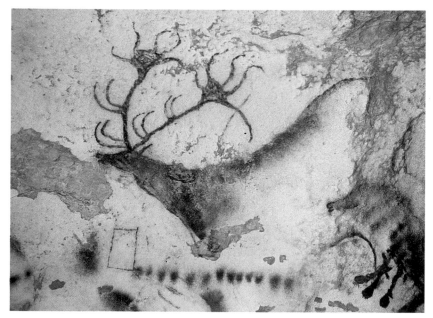

Seventeen thousand years ago, an Ice Age hunter crouched in the near darkness of a cavern in southwestern France. From a small leather pouch, he poured a handful of yellow powder into a stone dish. He dribbled some water onto the powder and stirred it with a stick to make a runny paste. Dipping a piece of fur into the yellow paste, he turned toward the rock face and began dabbing colour within the charcoal outline of a wild horse. In the low, flickering light cast by the man's stone lamp, the horse almost seemed to gallop out of the rock.

When we look at such paintings now, we see the world as it was thousands of years ago—long extinct animals roaming across Europe, archers hunting wild boar in Spain and armed hunters chasing mountain sheep in California. We see communal hunts, solitary hunts, combats, domestic scenes and dream images.

All over the world, ancient people learned how to draw and paint and carve. Most of their art was rooted in magical or religious beliefs related to animals and hunting. Each region developed its own style of rock art, and many of the images are easy to reproduce with the help of stencils. On the facing page are stencil versions of some of the prehistoric art found in Europe, including the famous French caves at Lascaux.

Rock On!

These animals and the row of dancers, enlivened by modern colours, are adapted from California rock art of about 1,000 years ago. To paint the dancing figures on denim shorts, you need two stencils. Use the outside outline to make the first stencil, and paint it solid white. Then make a stencil of the skinny inner figures. Place it on top of the white print, and paint it bright pink. This gives you pink people outlined in white. To make the dancers look really bouncy, stencil something to represent the ground, such as a row of triangles. Leave a space between this "ground" and the dancers' feet, and they will look as though they are dancing on air.

1 Dab two colours of paint onto the mat board. Lay a wrinkled piece of plastic wrap over the wet paint, and "smoosh" it around with your fingers.

4 For another style of pin, paint the mat board with a bright colour. Glue a torn piece of speckled or handmade paper to the front.

These brightly clothed figures are modelled after petroglyphs (pictures chipped into rock) found in California. The originals appear in elaborate costumes, carrying ceremonial objects. The running hunters are thousands of years older and are from Spanish rock art. Use these figures as they are for cards, enlarge them for T-shirts or reduce them for jewellery. You can make delightful pins by stencilling on mat board, modelling clay, salt dough, balsa wood or even small, flat pebbles.

2 Peel off the plastic wrap, and let the paint dry. Then glue the mat board to a slightly larger piece painted solid black.

5 First, stencil a figure in solid black. Then stencil a pattern, such as this green zigzag stripe, on top of the black figure.

3 Stencil a figure onto the pin with black paint. Because these figures are complicated, you must take extra care when cutting them.

6 Attach a pin to the back with a glue gun, or use a peel-and-stick pin. Let the paint dry for a few days. Finish with a coat of acrylic varnish.

If you have ever walked through an art museum or past the windows of a commercial art gallery, you will soon realize that you don't have to have a talent for realistic painting in order to be artistic. And guess what? You don't even have to be "artistic" to have fun with your own stencil designs. Look at the covers of your notebooks. They are probably filled with dozens of doodles. Try using some of them as stencil patterns. The stencils will do a real Cinderella act on your lowly doodles, turning them into clean, crisp, great-looking prints.

You may find out you're more artistic than you thought! We felt this doodle face had the right attitude toward forgotten homework and surprise tests, so we stencilled it on the flap of a school knapsack.

1 Stick this doodle face onto a piece of freezer paper with spray glue. Cut out the eyes and mouth with an X-acto knife.

2 With the pattern still on the freezer paper, cut out the head and hair in one piece. Be sure to keep the whole head intact. Save this cutout.

3 Stencil the head with white paint. If you are using a dark fabric, you might need more than one coat to cover it. Leave the stencil in place.

4 Stick the face stencil back into the shape it was cut from on the head stencil. Stencil the mouth and eyes black. Do the eyes carefully.

5 Remove both stencils. Be careful with the face stencil, because the spiral eyes are difficult to lift up without tearing.

Sources

Most of the materials used in this book should be easy to find. You can buy freezer paper in supermarkets. Hobby stores carry acrylic and fabric paints, spray adhesive (it might be called repositionable stencil adhesive), stencil brushes and X-acto knives. Hardware stores sell X-acto knives and latex paint. Sometimes, paint dealers offer latex "mistints" at a large discount. Some paint stores also carry foam rollers (they sell them for melamine paint).

If you can't find foam rollers, you can order them by mail from Buckingham Stencils, listed below, which also sells laser-cut Mylar stencils of most of the designs in this book.

General stencil supplies are available from the following sources. Most of these suppliers have catalogues and will fill mail orders.

Buckingham Stencils
205-66th Street
Tsawwassen, British Columbia
V4L 1M7
or
Ste. 1107-1468 Gulf Road
Point Roberts, Washington 98281

CANADA
Basat House Stencilling
1591 Grousewood Crescent
Kingston, Ontario K7L 5H6

The Cloth Shop
4415 West 10th Avenue
Vancouver, British Columbia
V6R 2H8

Damask Designs Inc.
3610 West 4th Avenue
Vancouver, British Columbia
V6R 1P1

Kindred Spirit
541½ Fisgard Street
Victoria, British Columbia V8W 1R3

Lee Valley Tools Ltd.
1080 Morrison Drive
Ottawa, Ontario K2H 8K7

Maiwa Handprints
6-1666 Johnston Street
Granville Island
Vancouver, British Columbia
V6H 3S2

Piety Ridge Primitives
15 Keele Street
King City, Ontario L0G 1K0

Stencilling by Leslie
7 Morgen Place
Nanaimo, British Columbia
V9T 5B8

UNITED STATES
Adele Bishop
Box 3349
Kinston, North Carolina 28501

American Traditional Stencils
Lower Bow Street RD 281
Northwood, New Hampshire
03261

The Great Wall
37050 Meadowbrook Common
#303
Fremont, California 94536

Plaid Enterprises (Simply Stencils)
Box 7600
Norcross, Georgia 30091-7600

Stencil Ease
Box 1127
Old Saybrook, Connecticut 06475

Stencil Magic (Delta)
2550 Pellissier Place
Whittier, California 90601-1505

Stenciler's Emporium Inc.
Box 536
9261 Ravenna Road B7
Twinsburg, Ohio 44087

Thanks to Binney & Smith (Lindsay, Ontario), makers of Crayola hobby paints; to Delta Technical Coatings, Inc. (Whittier, California), makers of Ceramcoat acrylic paints; and to Image Group (Vancouver) and AJM International (Montreal) for their combined efforts in getting us a pink cap just in time.

Throughout this book, I used many brands of paint, including Ceramcoat, Crayola, Setacolor, Liquitex, FabTex, Adele Bishop, DecoArt, Benjamin Moore, General Paint, Para Paint and Color Your World.